Edited
with an
introduction
by
R. H.
Hubbard

Production by
Gail Low

THOMAS DAVIES IN EARLY CANADA

By the eighteenth century topography, the delineation of place, was well mixed up with soldiering in both England and Europe. Before the advent of photography drawing was the only means of making military records. Officers' academies employed artists to teach their cadets to draw. Surveying and map-making likewise required the services of draughtsmen. As these activities called for the utmost fidelity to nature most topographical artists felt obliged to pursue one of the twin goals of the Renaissance to the exclusion of the other. As they usually chose naturalism over idealism their art seldom rose above the level of a craft.

Only in England was the situation such as to lead to new developments. That a few artists there managed to elevate topographical drawing into an art is usually attributed to the demand that existed for views of country houses and estates. This demand was at first satisfied by drawings that were merely heightened with white or enlivened with touches of colour; for as often as not they were intended for the engraver. It took Paul Sandby, who was trained in surveying, to progress from these to actual painting in water-colour. Gainsborough called him "the only man of genius" who had painted "real views of Nature in this country." His transparent views of Windsor Castle, dating from the seventeen-sixties and seventies, have been described by Mr. Ellis Waterhouse (quoting Gainsborough) as "the first 'real views of nature' to form the bulk of the achievement of a considerable artist."[1] The trend that Sandby began came to a climax half a century later in the grand nature art of Constable.

By the late eighteenth century there was, however, another side to English landscape art in water-colour. Artists like Alexander and John Robert Cozens, following the classical tradition of Claude Lorraine, who was so highly esteemed in England, cultivated the poetic and the sublime and prepared the way for Turner and his "golden visions."

Thomas Davies occupies a place in the history of water-colour painting close to that of Paul Sandby, his contemporary and almost certainly his friend. His art reached its peak at about the same time as Sandby's; but whereas the latter was a professional artist frequenting London, Windsor and the great houses of the land, the former was a professional soldier and only a leisure-time artist. His landscape painting was done mostly on his postings abroad.

His lack of formal training and his amateur standing had the great advantage of allowing him to give full rein to that "young fresh unspoiled vision" that marks him as an original.[2] He has been loosely designated by someone as "an eighteenth-century Rousseau *le douanier*"; for though his perspective and drawing of figures are a little faulty and his vision naive his technique of painting is not. The fulness of his handling of the water-colour medium is almost unrivalled. Breaking with the tradition of the tinted drawing, he painted directly on white paper in a full range of pure, rich colours. And though his spatial arrangements and placing of figures are occasionally Sandby-like, and his compositions occasionally reminiscent of those of John Robert Cozens, he was no one's follower.

Davies was not the first topographical artist to work in Canada. During the French régime military artists were responsible for a considerable body of drawings of the fortifications at Quebec and Louisbourg, and many of these are still to be found in the various official archives of Paris. Maps of the period often included miniature views of the towns of New France. But it was the British colonial period that saw the greatest proliferation of views, probably because the period of the conquest coincided with the rise of romanticism and the growing taste for pictures of far-off places. Two amateur artists were attached to Wolfe's force in 1759. Hervey Smyth, one of Wolfe's aides-de-camp, made drawings of the campaign in the Gulf of St. Lawrence, and Richard Short, purser of HMS *Prince of Orange*, views of Halifax and Quebec. Both are known for sets of engravings; the original drawings have disappeared.

Davies worked in Canada in the seventeen-fifties and sixties and again in the eighties. James Peachey, surveyor-general of Canada, was his contemporary in Quebec. George Heriot, deputy post-master-general of British North America, and James Pattison Cockburn, a lieutenant-colonel in the artillery, came after him, both like him having been trained at Woolwich and both pupils of Paul Sandby. These last two carried into the nineteenth century a practice that was to continue until the withdrawal of the British garrison from Canada in the early eighteen-seventies. They travelled throughout the province, painting on the spot, and did much to establish the primacy of landscape painting in Canadian

continues page 14

A view of Halifax harbour from Cornwallis (now McNab's) Island. It includes the Citadel and, just to the left of it, St. Paul's Church. "This new settlement is on a declivity . . . hanging like seats in a theatre, down to the water's edge; which view of the town from the river, with an incampment of the grenadiers from the 40th, 45th and 47th regiments, formed on the hill close by the citadel above the town, together with the neighbouring verdant woods on every side, and some few buildings on George's island (which is conveniently situated for defence as well as ornament) affords one of the most delightful prospects that can possibly be conceived" (Knox, 1 July, 1757).

A view (above) of the siege of Louisbourg in 1758. This drawing is said to be a repetition of a lost original. The photographs pasted on the upper corners are of the two sides of the Louisbourg medal. The inscription includes a key to the letters on the drawing. "Fire was brisk on our side," wrote Amherst on 24 July, 1758. "Col. Williamson silenced their Guns and burnt a part of the Barracks last night which we had better not have done. The Town looked very much in ruins." At right, the plundering and burning of Grimross (now Gagetown) on the St. John River. "It being late in the Day, I gave orders for Burning the Houses & Barns, being about 50 in all & destroying all the Grain of which there was a good deal & Every thing else that could be of the least Service to the Inhabitants hereafter" (Monckton, 3–4 November, 1758).

Amherst (above) before Ticonderoga in 1759. "About ten o'clock," he wrote, a Deserter came in & said the Garrison was to get off and blow up the Fort . . . and soon we saw the Fort on fire and an Explosion." Fort Frederick (right) was on the site of the modern city of Saint John. Monckton landed here in September 1758 and met with no opposition.

11

The two drawings at left, both of which come from Lord Amherst's collection, show the ruins of Fort Frédéric at Crown Point, New York. "The fort," Kalm writes, "is built on a rock, consisting of black lime-slates ... it is nearly quadrangular, has high and thick walls, made of the same lime-stone, of which there is a quarry about half a mile from the fort. On the eastern part of the fort, is a high tower [shown here in ruins], which is proof against bombshells, provided with very thick and substantial walls, and well stored with cannon, from the bottom almost to the very top; and the governor lives in the tower. In the terre-plein of the fort is a well built little church, and houses of stone for the officers and soldiers." Fort Frédéric was situated at the southern end of Lake Champlain, on a neck of land between the lake and the river. "There are sharp rocks on all sides towards the land," Kalm tells us, "beyond a cannon-shot from the fort, but among them there are some which are as high as the walls of the fort, and very near them." A new fortress was begun by Amherst and completed in late November 1759. It shows in the scene at right, which comes from the Derby collection and which is a finished version of the drawing at lower left, to which the new buildings have been added. Construction was under way in August, when Amherst wrote, "400 men at work on the ground where the Fort is to be, the first situation I think I have seen in America that is no where commanded. It will have all the advantages of the Lake and of the situation of Ground that can be wished for." Three months later he brought the work to an end: "Very bad weather, but I must put the fortress in a good situation for defence and to cover the Garrison before I leave it." The English called the fortress Crown Point.

13

art.

Davies was the best of them all. Though no direct influence on later art can be claimed for him—his works were hidden away in private collections—his perception of nature was such as to place him in the central tradition of Canadian art. His work had "a brilliance, breadth and clarity not to be associated again with the Canadian landscape until more than a century and a half later with the advent of the Group of Seven."[3]

In spite of the occasional reference to him in books and periodicals and though a few of his works were early acquired by museums and libraries (notably the Public Archives of Canada under Sir Arthur Doughty) Davies remained an obscure name until 1953. In that year a collection of more than 50 of his views was sold at Christie's from the Earl of Derby's library at Knowsley.[4] Though a London art critic judged him to be of "no exceptional talent" and described his drawings as having only the "interest of showing what Niagara Falls looked like before the American War of Independence,"[5] the lot was sold for a high price for the time. The purchaser, a London dealer in views, divided it into two main saleable portions. An "American" group went to dealers in New York and twenty "Canadian" views were bought by the National Gallery of Canada in 1954. It is amusing to note that a Londoner's hazy idea of North American geography resulted in the New-York Historical Society's acquiring the two scenes of Niagara Falls in the Derby collection and the National Gallery of Canada's receiving the only one of the Genesee River in the state of New York. Others of the American views, together with the Gibraltar and West Indian groups, were bought by the Royal Ontario Museum in Toronto, which heeded the advice of its pioneer keeper of Canadiana, the late F. St. George Spendlove, that "every original drawing by Thomas Davies should be recorded, and should be regarded as a national treasure."[6]

In 1956 *Canadian Art* published companion articles on Davies by Colonel C.P. Stacey and Miss Kathleen M. Fenwick establishing his biography and his place in the history of art.[7] Since then the drawings in the National Gallery have been exhibited and reproduced, and in 1970 work was begun on the first complete exhibition of Davies' work. In the course of the preliminary research for this exhibition additional biographical material has been found,

14

mainly by Colonel Stacey.[8] A number of drawings have been added to Davies' *oeuvre*, which is now full enough to allow a stylistic development to be traced. But there are still significant gaps in our knowledge. Further letters and a portrait might confirm the existing impression of him as a kindly and helpful man, a lover of nature and of sport and a gentleman amateur of science.

Two aspects of his contribution appear important. He is first of all an iconographer of North America. All his views permit of as exact an identification as is possible in drawings of the period. Brimful of authentic details of places and of the houses, costumes and occupations of the people, they correspond remarkably well with the written descriptions of more or less contemporary travellers such as Peter Kalm, Isaac Weld, George Heriot (the artist) and Joseph Bouchette. The one anomaly is that such a naturalist as Davies should have been so inexact in his definition of botanical detail: his drawing of trees and plants has a period conventionality that is at odds with the precise delineation of his bird drawings. In the case of his more strictly military drawings there are appropriate passages in the papers of Lord Amherst, General Robert Monckton, Colonel George Williamson and Captain John Knox, all contemporaries of his.

The main difficulty encountered in the study of Davies' drawings is in their dating. In spite of an inscription such as "taken on the spot 1766," any given view may in fact be later in date, having been sketched in that year and painted later. Indeed, some of the drawings are inscribed with a military rank Davies did not attain until some years later than the inscribed date. Here stylistic analysis must be called in to help in establishing a chronology.

The second aspect of Davies most deserving of our attention is the aesthetic quality of his work. The style he evolved is that of an essentially untrained artist elaborated in its highest degree of decorative stylization. The results are to my mind finer and more satisfying than the works of Henri Rousseau a century later.

Three distinct manners emerge from a study of the development of Davies' style. The first is diagrammatic, the essential mode of the military draughtsman. The second is a picturesque manner that clearly echoes the cosmopolitan art of the eighteenth century and appears in the work of most artists of the rococo age in some form or other. These first two manners appear in his earlier work, 15

continues page 17

The drawing below is taken from a sheet containing a plan, elevation (shown here) and section of one of the row-galleys built by Amherst and his men in 1760 for use on Lake Ontario. Two such galleys can be seen in action on page 19. "I employed," writes Amherst, "all the carpenters that could be picked out of all the troops in repairing the batteaus, building the boats to carry the 12 Pounders .... I ordered a Hautwitzer on board the Row Galley that was intended for a 12 Pounder .... The five Row Galleys had four heavy twelves & one Hautwitzer." These galleys, according to the inscription in

Davies' own hand, were designed "to Row with 22 Oars besides Main-sail and Fore-sail on Occasion, to be mounted with one 18 or 12 Pounder for a Chase two 6 or 4 Pounders .... This Vessel in its Construction will partake of the Advantages of a Galley or Zebeque in its Agility, and of a Sloop in its Sailing and defence with the addition of a Prow for Boarding or Landing." The three drawings at right are military diagrams, probably made during the winter of 1759–60, when Amherst's army was in New York. They show various military formations and lines of fire.

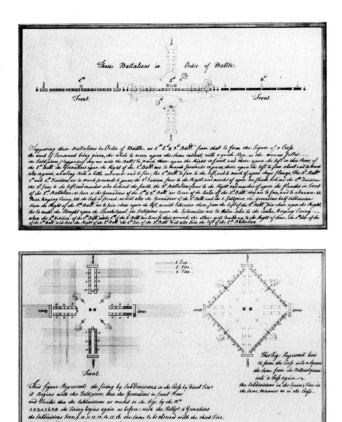

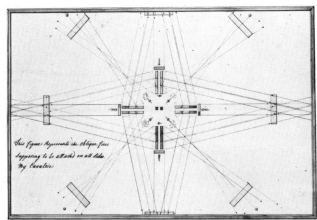

sometimes in combination. But they alone could never have accounted for the quality and originality I have ascribed to him. The third, his mature style, was his own creation, absorbing the other two but rising far above them. In this ultimate manner his drawing is so delicate and minute, his colours so pure and fresh, his light so clear and bright, his water so crystalline, that everything in a picture seems to take on an eternal verity. Yet his was no ideal world like that of the "southern" school of English water-colourists. Davies' affinities are to the manuscript illuminators of the early fifteenth century, with their charming realism, or to the Flemish artists of the seventeenth century in their pictures of an earthly paradise.

The present portfolio of reproductions of Davies' water-colours, assembled from collections on two continents, will illustrate both his military career and his artistic development. Omitting the English scenes and those of Madeira, Gibraltar and the West Indies, it represents (with trivial exceptions) the entire body of his work in North America as it is now known.

Thomas Davies was born in or about 1737: his obituary notice in the *Gentleman's Magazine* states that he was in his 75th year when he died in 1812. His birthplace was probably Shooter's Hill, where his father David Davies lived; the family was doubtless of Welsh origin. Shooter's Hill lies just above Woolwich, seat of the Royal Military Academy, which trained officers for the Royal Artillery and the Royal Engineers.

In 1755, when he was about eighteen, Davies entered Woolwich as a gentleman cadet in the artillery. He took lessons from the Gamaliel Massiot who was drawing master from 1744 until succeeded by Paul Sandby in 1768. In 1756, the year in which the Seven Years' War broke out, Davies was appointed lieutenant fireworker, the lowest commissioned rank in the artillery. The following year, at twenty or so, he was promoted second lieutenant and sent with an artillery detachment on his first posting overseas. Sailing from England in the spring, he accompanied the abortive expedition against Louisbourg which, after failing to draw the French out of port, retired to Halifax.

Very soon after arriving at Halifax in July Davies drew his first Canadian picture, *A View of Hallifax in Nova Scotia* (page 7), showing "a Squadron going off [to] Louisbourgh." From Corn-

continues page 20

Top left, another view of Crown Point, taken from the northeast. The southwest aspect of Ticonderoga at lower left is another version of the water-colour on page 10. The view of the action off Fort La Galette above, with the marvellous sunflowers in the left foreground, was made from the site of the modern town of Ogdensburg, looking across the St. Lawrence to where Prescott now stands. "The General did me the Honour," Williamson recalls, "to accept of my offer to attack the French man with my 5 Galley's: we got to within random Shot of her but falling dark we deferred the undertaking untill the Grey of the next morning the 17th. when we contrived it so well that in 2 hours & 1/2 she struck to my red Flag . . . the General as a Compliment to my endeavours was pleased to Name the Prize the Williamson Frigate."

wallis (now McNab's) Island he presents a distant view of the young city with reasonably accurate if very tiny representations of the Citadel, St. Paul's Church and a cluster of houses by the harbour's edge, the same view that Knox describes as affording "one of the most delightful prospects that can possibly be conceived." In spite of a certain dulness in tone and dryness in the drawing, Davies has here hit upon a combination of diagrammatic accuracy and decorative treatment that sets the tone for the later development of his style.

In 1758, having apparently wintered in New York, he joined General Jeffery Amherst's successful expedition to Louisbourg. The diagrammatic view he made of the *Siege of Louisbourgh* (page 8),[9] with letters and an explanatory key, surveys a wide panorama including the town and the chateau—now so impressively restored—half-hidden in smoke, French ships in harbour, the battery at Lighthouse Point and the British forces attacking by land and sea.

By the autumn Davies was with Monckton's force laying waste the Acadian settlements on the St. John River. His monochrome drawing of the *Plundering and Burning of the City of Grymross* (page 9) is a lurid nocturne that records the destruction of every farm and every building at Grimross, now called Gagetown. He passed the winter at the new fort Monckton had built to replace Fort La Tour after capturing it in September. *A North View of Fort Frederick* (page 11), taken from Navy Island in Saint John harbour, shows the troops encamped on the hill behind the fort just as Monckton himself described the scene.

In the spring of 1759, having been promoted first lieutenant, Davies returned to New York and there joined the Lake Champlain expedition commanded by Amherst, the newly appointed commander-in-chief in America. In June he evidently witnessed the army mustering at Lake George, a lost view of which he exhibited at the Royal Academy in 1774. In July Ticonderoga fell easily to Amherst. Davies' on-the-spot diagram, *The Lines and Fort of Ticonderoga* (page 10) is artistically unambitious. It shows Lake Champlain with the ruins of Fort Carillon as blown up by the French, the British redoubts and the lines where Abercromby had been defeated in 1758. The amusing detail in the foreground—an Indian stalking a porcupine—may be taken to indicate a growing interest in wildlife.

continues page 24

*The drawing at top left shows
the passage of Amherst's men
down the rapids at Montreal.
The men had little experience
with boats and more than a hundred
were lost. "Set out for Isle
de Montreal this Day," Williamson
writes in his matter-of-fact way,
"& arrived there the 6th in the
evening with little opposition,
but in passing the several Rifts
& Falls, we had upwards of 100 men
drowned several Batteaus with
Provisions Artillery, &c Stores
lost as our Coup required the utmost
Expedn." Sir Joshua Reynolds,
the great English portrait painter,
used this drawing for his*

*well-known portrait of Amherst
and later apparently folded it
carelessly and put it in his pocket.
The creases are still visible.
His collector's mark is stamped
at the lower right corner and is
reproduced at far left.
The view at lower left
is of the upper falls
on the Genesee River (Davies calls it
the Senesca River) at what is now
Rochester, New York. Heriot
gives a full description of the
scene: about six miles above
Lake Ontario "a fall of sixty feet
in altitude, and occupying
the whole breadth of the river,
obtrudes itself on the view
and commands the admiration
of the traveller . . . . On
pursuing the channel
still higher up,
many rapids and cascades
present themselves."*

Above, a view of Niagara from just above the Horseshoe Falls,
looking toward the American side. Early travellers, like Kalm,
were deeply impressed by this sight. "One cannot help," he wrote,
"being amazed and awed when standing above the cataract gazing down . . . .
In its descent, near the bottom, the water strikes the rock in some places
and there it foams and roars in gigantic leaps . . . with a heavy,
persistent and hastily appearing mist dashing forth;
for the liquid is creamy white and looks like a thick vapour. When falling,
the water at the top first appears green; but further down
it takes on a snow white tinge . . . . When the water reaches the bottom
it sets all in motion beneath it, so that it swirls about in circles
and whirls like the liquid in a seething cauldron . . . . On a certain time
of the day when the sun is shining, we can always see a rainbow against
the mist." The picturesque scene at right is of Montreal,
taken from St. Helen's Island. Buildings visible in the picture
include the Récollet church, the parish church and the fort.

23

Later in the summer the army advanced to Crown Point. The Public Archives of Canada possess two monochrome panoramas of the place (page 12) showing old Fort Frédéric in ruins. The finished and coloured drawing, *A South View of . . . Crown Point* (page 13) adds the new fort that Amherst completed very late in the year. Military drawings such as these take minor liberties with realistic detail, showing full reflections on water, for example, but few shadows on land—where presumably they might have interfered with topographical accuracy.

By this time, as is stated in the often inaccurate "Statement of Services"[10] that Davies made late in life, he was "Bateaux Master for the Artillery Department" and commanded a small fleet on Lake Champlain. It was probably at this time that he made a monochrome drawing of *A Rock 25 Miles WNW of Crown Point*, the lengthy description on which indicates that he was sent to investigate a rock face that at a distance resembled a waterfall.[11] This was one of a series of exploratory trips on which Amherst appears to have employed his officers during periods of inactivity in the slow-moving campaign. Too late to be of any help to Wolfe at Quebec, he turned back in the late autumn and wintered in New York.

It was probably during that winter that Davies drew a set of military diagrams for the general. One of these, dated 1759, is the *Plan, Elevation and Section of a Galliot* (page 16). The craft represented is a row-galley equipped with a single gun, of the sort that was to be built on Lake Ontario the following summer. There are also three technical diagrams of battle formations (page 17).

In the spring of 1760 a campaign was mounted against Montreal, which was still in French hands. By July Amherst had arrived at Oswego and by mid-August embarked a force on Lake Ontario. Davies again was Bateaux Master and himself commanded one of the row-galleys that attacked a French vessel, the *Outaouaise*, which had been built at "Pointe-au-Baril" (now Maitland, Ontario). Both Amherst and his artillery commander, Colonel George Williamson, have left descriptions of this action, which took place at the modern site of Ogdensburg, New York. Davies portrays the action in the background of a fine water-colour, *A View of Fort La Galet* (page 19). The picture also includes some not-very-warlike Indians (probably those of Père François Picquet's mission at La Galette) and some giant sunflowers, which adorn the left foreground.

This was the 17th of August. A few days later Fort Lévis on Ile Royale at the head of the rapids fell to the English and left the way open to Montreal. A workmanlike monochrome of the *Passage of the Army . . . down the Rapids of St. Lawrence* (page 21) bears Sir Joshua Reynolds' collector's mark (page 20) and the folds for which the first president of the Royal Society may have been responsible, having stuffed the drawing into his pocket after using it to paint the scene into the background of his famous portrait of Amherst. The shocking loss in the rapids of several boats and more than a hundred men was due (according to George Heriot writing many years later) to the inexperience of the pilots.

On the 6th of September the army was encamped before Montreal. On the 8th the city and with it New France capitulated to Amherst. On the 9th, according to Williamson's account of the affair, Davies headed an officers' party of artillery accompanied by a "Band of Musick," which entered the fort. He was almost certainly the officer who first hoisted the British flag over Montreal to the accompaniment of "three Cheers . . . answer'd by our Parade."

But he did not stay there long. Before winter closed in he was exploring the St. Lawrence and Lake Ontario and thence returned to New York by way of Lake Oneida. From 1760 come additional views of Ticonderoga and Crown Point (page 18), which may have been drawn at this time or based on sketches made the previous year.

His travels were resumed in 1761, when he explored the south shore of Lake Ontario and visited Indian tribes. One result of the journey is a long, narrow map, *Draught of the River St. Lawrence*, which indicates the various channels from Lake Ontario to Montreal.[12] Another is a monochrome drawing heightened with sepia, *A South View of the great Falls of Senesca River in Lake Ontario* (page 21) representing not a fall on the Seneca River but the uppermost of three cataracts near the mouth of the Genesee, then in Seneca country. This picturesque scene of the fall, which Heriot was to describe as pouring "with plaintive sound" and producing "a curtain of resplendent whiteness," was engraved and

25

continues page 33

Greenbush, a settlement on the east bank of the Hudson River (above), was founded in 1631
when Killian van Rensselaer bought a tract of land there from the Indians.
This view was probably taken from the southern part of the present-day Albany.
The two houses (centre and right) are Fort Crailo and Douw's Point.
Fort Crailo was the van Rensselaer homestead and is still standing;
Douw's Point was the home of a mayor of Albany
in the eighteenth century but has since been demolished.
The serene landscape at right is of Flushing on Long Island. That part of the island,
Weld tells us, was then crowded with villas "and although the face of the country
is here flat and sandy, devoid of trees, and wholly uninteresting . . . here are
several considerable towns, as, Flatbush, Jamaica, Brooklyn, Flushing."

27

28

A south view of Passaic Falls (left) near Paterson, New Jersey. "The course
of that river through rocks," La Rochefoucault later wrote,
"presents a grand spectacle . . . . On the day I visited it the sun shone bright;
the weather was hot, the wind pretty high;
all which circumstances combined to give great beauty
to this magnificent scene." Weld has also left a description
of the falls: the river "suddenly precipitates itself,
in one entire sheet, over a ledge of rocks of nearly eighty feet
in perpendicular height; below it runs on through a chasm,
formed of immense rocks on each side; they are higher than the fall,
and seem to have been once united together." Note the elegant couple
under a parasol at the top of the cliff. Fort Edward was the starting-point
on the portage between the Hudson and Lake Champlain. Davies owned land
in the vicinity and the cataract (above)
was a short distance downstream.

Otter Creek rises in the hills of Vermont and empties into Lake Champlain
to the north of Crown Point.
The view above dates from 1766.
Amherst mentions in his journal
that he sent a certain Captain Johnson to explore the Otter.
"He found eight falls instead of three," he notes,
"and mostly very bad ones;
the sides of the River for the most part swampy,
and he says the most impracticable impassible River that he ever saw."
Like the drawing on page 21, the view at right shows the highest
of the three falls on the Genesee River at Rochester, New York.
Davies calls the river by its old name, the Casconchiagon.
Heriot saw the fall; it "pours," he recalled,
"with a plaintive sound, over a rock almost perpendicular,
and, broken amid the variety of its movements,
produces a curtain of resplendent whiteness."
Note the fall colouring in the background and the Indian family,
picked out in brilliant detail in the left foreground.

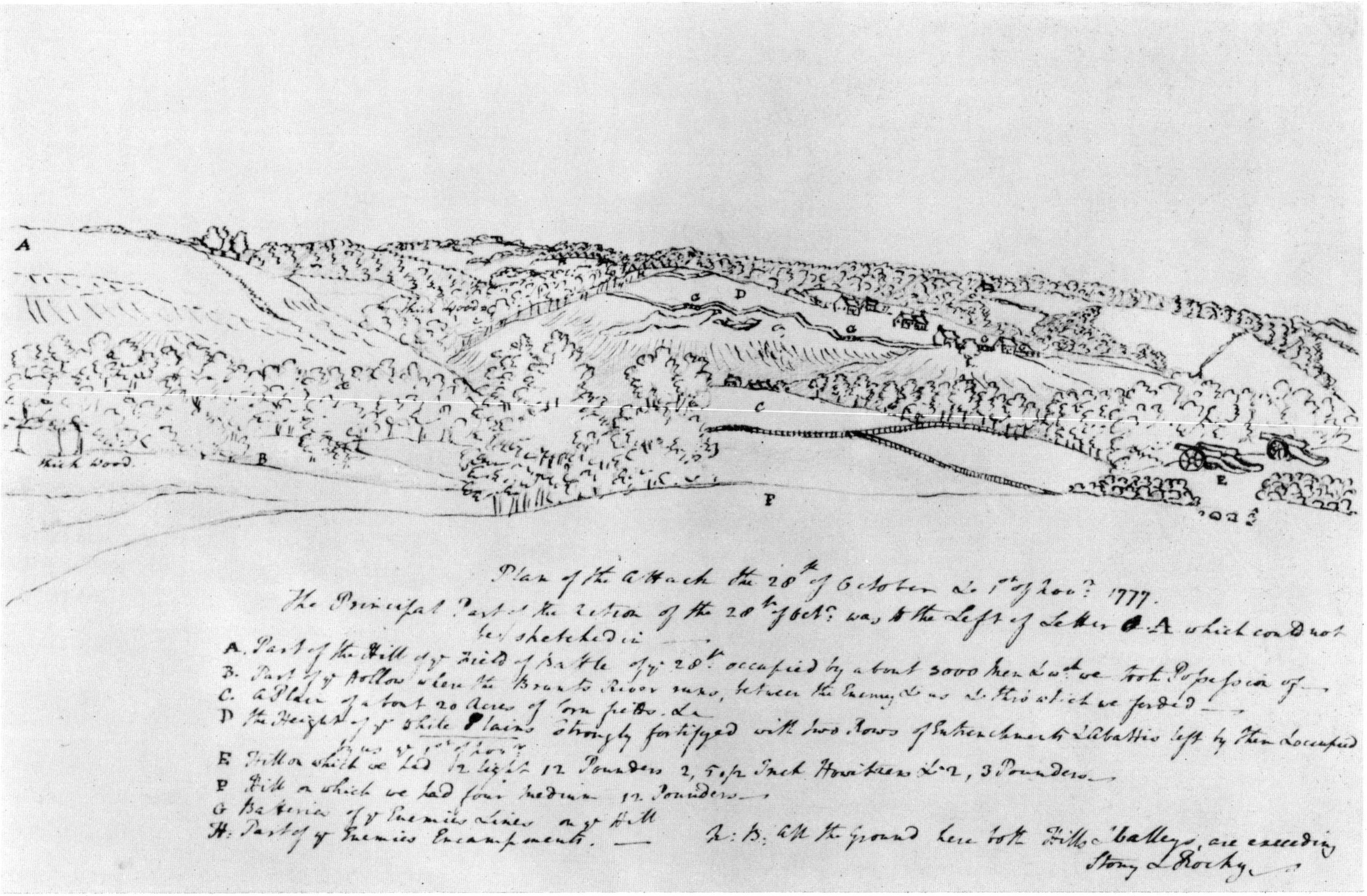

Plan of the Attack the 20th of October and 1st of Nov.r 1777.

The Principal Part of the Retreat of the 28th of Oct.r was to the Left of Letter A. which con.d not
be sketched in

A. Part of the Hill of y.e Field of Battle.
B. Part of y.e Hollow where the Brunx River runs, between the Enemy & us & this which we forded
C. A Place of about 20 acres of Corn fields &c.
D. The Heights of White Plains strongly fortified with two Rows of Intrenchments & Abattis left by them & occupied
E. Hill on which we had 2 light 12 Pounders 2, 5½ Inch Howitzers & 2, 3 Pounders.
P. Hill on which we had four medium 12 Pounders.
G. Batteries of y.e Enemies Lines on y.e Hill
H. Part of y.e Enemies Encampments. —

N.B. All the ground here took with the Valleys, are exceeding
Stony & Rocky.

AMBASSADOR & MRS. J. WILLIAM MIDDENDORF II

This drawing of the battle of White Plains, which took place in 1776, is probably Davies' work. Davies was there, as he himself recalls,
"with a brigade of guns." In the two views at right Davies returns to the great scene he had already treated once before (see page 22),
depicting the falls at Niagara from above and below the cataract on the Canadian side. "Here," Weld reports, "great numbers
of the bodies of fishes, squirrels, foxes, and various other animals" that have been carried over the falls
"are washed up . . . . A dreadful stench arises from the quantity of putrid matter lying on the shore, and numberless birds of prey,
attracted by it, are always seen hovering about the place."
One of these birds can be seen in the upper picture at right.

published in London a few years later as one of a series of *Six Views of Waterfalls* dedicated to Amherst. It includes the figure of an artist, doubtless Davies himself, and in the foreground some luxuriant plantains of a kind that recur in his work, as well as a highly stylized tree of indeterminate species.

After another winter in New York Davies made a further journey of exploration in 1762, this time to Lake George, Lake Champlain and on to Montreal. Dating from this trip is a schematic yet picturesque *East View of the Great Cataract of Niagara* (page 22), a rendering of the scene that evoked such "wonder and astonishment" in visitors like the Swedish botanist Pater Kalm. With its two Indians in the foreground, it was also engraved in the *Six Views of Waterfalls*. The drawing is notable for an inscribed note, "The Variety of Colours in the Woods shews the true Nature of the Country." Though not a particularly brilliant display of autumn colours, this may well be their first appearance in a painting. Also dated 1762 is a fine *View of Montreal in Canada* (page 23) seen from St. Helen's Island—according to Heriot the most favourable aspect. Typifying the picturesque style to perfection, the drawing presents the town from behind an elegant reclining couple under trees spun over with fretted vines in true eighteenth-century fashion. The buildings in the background include the Récollet church, the parish church (predecessor of the Notre Dame of today) and the fort. The walled city is surrounded by those "charming meadows, and delightful woods" observed by Kalm some few years before.

Making their appearance just at this point, two views of the island of Martinique, dated 1762 and now in the Mariners Museum, Newport News, give rise to a problem in Davies' chronology—in view of his northern water-colours of that same year and of his own statement that he spent the winter of 1761–62 in New York. For that was the very period of Monckton's expedition to Martinique: Fort Royal fell in February 1762. These delicately-painted diagrammatic views of Fort Royal and Saint-Pierre must therefore have been based on the work of some other artist who accompanied the force. The same would apply to Davies' *Plan of the Havanna*, dated 1762, in the John Carter Brown Library in Providence; there is no evidence that he took part in the siege of Havana.

By March 1762, in fact, he was in command of an artillery detachment in New York, having just been promoted captain lieutenant. In 1763, at the end of the war, he returned to England but was back in New York the following year. The next few years, he states, were spent "in New York and Canada." The style of the water-colours he painted on his travels in the year or two after his return make it fair to assume that he had met Paul Sandby in England or at least been influenced by his work. *A View near Flushing, on Long Island* (a resort of rich New Yorkers in the eighteenth century) is dated 1765. It has a broad horizontal composition (page 27) and an altogether more developed technique that is close to that of the father of British water-colour. *A View of Green Bush on the Hudsons River near Albany* (page 26), dated 1766, is another spacious and rather pale landscape. Behind two officers and their affectionate dog Davies shows the village of Greenbush, now called Rensselaer, opposite Albany. Fort Crailo, the old Van Rensselaer house, is one of the two houses shown in the picture.

A view on the upper Hudson, *The Cataract . . . near Fort Edward* (page 29), where Davies himself held land, gives evidence of a return to the picturesque style of earlier years and a turning away from Sandby's direct influence. The same applies to several other views sketched on his second North American tour. But a series of waterfalls, either dated or datable in 1766, also reveals a notable development of style and technique. The first two, *A South View of the Pisaiack Falls* (page 28) — Passaic Falls in New Jersey—and *A View of the Falls of Otter Creek* (page 30), a scene near Lake Champlain, have the playfully irregular compositions that are typical of the eighteenth century, as well as Davies' usual array of fishermen. But in contrast to the *Montreal* view of 1762, they exhibit a new and decorative use of wiry line.

A View of the Casconchiagon or Great Seneca Falls (page 31) goes even further. With its Indian family reposing in the foreground, it shows the same scene on the Genesee as the monochrome view of 1761. But here the masterful breadth in the handling of the water-colour medium is so much in the mode of the mature style, which still lay in the future, as to belie the inscribed date. The glow of autumn colour in this work equals that of the Quebec water-colours of the seventeen-eighties. Probably the scene was sketched in 1766 and painted twenty years later.

34

Two splendid undated views of Niagara Falls, that wonder of wonders, appear to have been made at this time. *Niagara Falls from Above* (page 33) possesses a finely-balanced composition and a great distinction in the drawing. It generally illustrates Heriot's effusive prose—"the effect is awfully grand, magnificent and sublime"—and more particularly Weld's gruesome note about the birds of prey that hovered in wait for animals washed over the falls. *Niagara Falls from Below* (page 33), with its great curtains of spray, likewise exemplifies that spaciousness, that glassiness of the water, that solidity of the rocks which are the hallmarks of Davies' maturing style.

In 1767 (in spite of the date 1769 in the "Statement of Services") Davies returned to England. This time he could hardly help meeting Sandby, who in 1768 was appointed drawing master at Woolwich. That was also the year in which Sandby became one of the founders of the Royal Academy; and frequently, from 1769 onwards, he served on its hanging committees. If, as seems likely, he and Davies were friends it was no accident that the latter was a fairly regular "Honorary Exhibitor" at the Academy. Davies first exhibited in 1771, when he was also promoted captain and appointed to command a new company of artillery at Woolwich. His offerings at the Academy were three flower-pieces: "wild plants collected in North America," "the horn plant of Detroit" and "a creeping cereus with a fly." A lost view of Springfield, Massachusetts, was shown in 1773, and views of Lake George and Crown Point (perhaps the one on page 13) appeared in 1774 and 1775 respectively.

Meanwhile, in 1773, on the eve of the American Revolution, Davies had embarked on a third North American tour of duty. By this time he was serving as unpaid aide-de-camp to Amherst. Arriving at Halifax, his company moved to Boston in 1774 and doubtless saw action at Bunker Hill in June 1775. After General Howe's evacuation of Boston in March 1776 and the subsequent withdrawal to Halifax, he joined in the descent on New York. Having made a will mentioning his wife Mary and his two children and properties in London and at Fort Edward, he took part in the battle of Long Island on the 27th of August and the ensuing entry into New York. At the battle of White Plains on the 28th of October he was in action "with a brigade of guns." I have   35

continues page 44

Two views of the attack on Fort Washington on 16 November, 1776. The drawing at left is an earlier version of the finished water-colour at right. Both are taken from the high ground on the opposite bank of the Harlem River. The Morris (Jumel) house just visible on the skyline at the far left is still standing. Davies himself explains the scene as follows: "On the Right hand on a hill in a thick wood, were posted two light twelves Commanded by Capt Rockford, & two 3 pdrs Hessian to scour the face of the hill to be storm'd by the two Hessian Collums, the Perl Frigate lay in the oppening to assist also. Next two Rebel Redouts to defend the hill. In the Center below a Battery of 4 twelve Pounders Comd. by Major Martin, part of Fort Washington appearing on the hill above, next two Rebell Redouts on the harlem Creek to prevent the Landing of the Guards & Light Infantry, where they soon effected their landing and took the Redouts, being Coverd by a Battery on the Right of four Medium 12 Poundrs Command by your humble Servant; lower down was a Mortar Battery of two 5 1/2 Inch Comd by Lt Collins, & lower still almost opposite Col: Morrisses house which also appears in the View, twenty odd pieces of light Artillery."

36

HENRY FRANCIS DU PONT WINTERTHUR MUSEUM

*The vigorous drawing at left shows the landing of the British forces in New Jersey on 20 November, 1776
under the command of Cornwallis.*
*The drawing was at first attributed to Lord Rawdon, later first Marquess of Hastings,
but is now believed to be by Davies, who is known to have been with Cornwallis
on his pursuit of Washington into New Jersey.*
*The water-colour of the Hudson River looking toward New York (above) was taken from Fort Knyphausen
in 1779. "We embarked," Weld notes, "on the second day of July, about two o'clock in the afternoon.
Scarcely a breath of air was stirring at the time; but the tide carried us up at the rate of
about two miles and a half an hour . . . . To describe all the grand and beautiful prospects
presented to the view on passing along this noble river would be an endless task."*
*During the British occupation Fort Washington was renamed in honour of General Wilhelm Knyphausen,
the Hessian commander of New York. Davies was there as commander of artillery in 1777 and 1778.*

*The drawing above was taken from a point near the Morris house (see page 36).
It shows New York just below the horizon, with Harlem Creek in the middle distance.
Note the cactus in the foreground. It was probably a piece of exotica
growing in the Morris grounds. The air is perfectly still, just as it was
for Weld. "The sky remained all day as serene as possible, and as the water
was perfectly smooth, it reflected in a most beautiful manner the images
of the various objects on the shore. The sun, setting in all his glory,
added fresh beauties to this calm and peaceable scene, and permitted us
for the last time to behold the distant spires of New York,
illumined by his parting rays." The water-colour at right is of Quebec
and was taken near Beauport Ferry, at the mouth of the St. Charles River,
in 1787. A number of details are recognizable, among them the cathedral,
the Hôtel-Dieu and the Récollet and Jesuit churches.
The temporary Citadel built by General Haldimand toward the end
of the American Revolution is visible above the walls at the north edge of town.
Just below it Davies himself can be observed, sketching the scene before him.*

42

The view at left is of the falls on the Chaudiere, four miles from Quebec. It includes another self-portrait and shows Davies dressed much as he was in the view of Quebec from Beauport Ferry, in a blue coat and black hat. Davies' painting corresponds closely with the eye-witness accounts we have. Heriot, for example, notes that the waters, "being separated by rocks, form three distinct cataracts, the largest of which is on the western side, and they unite, in the basin beneath, their broken and agitated waves. The form of the rock forces a part of the waters, into an oblique direction . . . . The cavities worn in the rocks, produce a pleasing variety, and cause the descending waters to revolve with foaming fury, to whose whiteness the gloomy cliffs, present a strong opposition of colour. The vapour from each division of the falls, quickly mounting through the air, bestows an enlivening beauty on the landscape." Bouchette comments that the "best view is to the left from a ledge of rocks that project into the basin; from this point the scene is surprisingly grand." Davies knew of this ledge too, for he has painted in the tiny figure of a fisherman standing on it, just at the foot of the falls. The rich and beautiful scene at right is of the village of Château-Richer, fifteen miles downriver from Quebec. "The farm-houses hereabouts," Kalm tells us, "are generally built along the rising banks of the river . . . and are about three or four arpens from each other. To some farms are annexed small orchards . . . however, almost every farmer has a kitchen garden . . . . The farm-houses are generally built of stone, but sometimes of timber . . . . The roofs are covered with boards, and the crevices and chinks are filled up with clay. Other farm buildings are covered with straw." Bouchette remarks that along this part of the river there is a continuous strip of saltmarsh a mile or so in width, visible here in the middle distance, which is full of game: "during the spring and autumn, the sportsman is sure to meet . . . wild-ducks, snipes, and plover, in amazing quantities."

attributed to him, on grounds of similarities in style and handwriting, a schematic pen drawing of the last engagement (page 32), which is misdated but fully annotated.

He was also in action when Fort Washington on the Hudson above New York fell to the British on the 16th of November. In a lengthy explanation of his original diagram of the battle, *A View of the Attack against Fort Washington* (page 36)—of which there is a finished version in the Winterthur Museum (page 37)—he notes the British and Hessians "scouring the hill," a glimpse of the Hudson with a British frigate firing, the fort at the summit with his own battery below and the Morris (Jumel) mansion, which still stands on the bank above the Harlem River. After this he accompanied Cornwallis' force in pursuit of Washington into New Jersey. A drawing attributed to him of *The Landing of the British Forces in the Jerseys* (page 38) shows troops and artillery scaling the heights on the far bank of the Hudson.

A few records survive of Davies' activities over the next two years. In 1777 he was posted to Fort Knyphausen (Fort Washington renamed for the Hessian commander of New York) in command of the artillery. There, in 1778, he wrote two letters to Amherst in England, sending his regards to Lady Amherst and generally indicating that he was on very friendly terms with the general. Congratulating Amherst on his appointment as commander-in-chief of the forces, he notes "with most Sincere and abundant thanks" that he has heard from his own "good little Woman" that Amherst has made him one of his paid aides-de-camp. In these years he painted two serene river landscapes with fishermen in the vicinity of the fort. *A View of New York, Long Island, etc., taken on Harlem Creek near Morris House* (page 40) is dated 1778 and discloses the spires of New York in the far distance. *A View on the Hudson River* (page 39) is dated the following year and looks down toward New York from Fort Knyphausen.

Early in 1779 he was back at Woolwich. Two drawings of the troops encamped in St. Jame's Park, London were painted after Amherst's suppression of the Gordon Riots. They are peaceful and pretty scenes with fashionable figures strolling beside the rows of tents and with glimpses of Whitehall and the Queen's House (Buckingham Palace) in their backgrounds. These formed part of George III's Topographical Collection, which was acquired by the

British Museum in 1828. Amherst owned a version of one of the two scenes.

In 1782 Davies became a major. The following year, which marked the end of the war, he was promoted lieutenant-colonel. He now ceased to be Amherst's aide-de-camp and took up command at Gibraltar. The fine series of·water-colours now in the Royal Ontario Museum includes one in which Davies reconstructs the famous siege of 1782 by the French and Spanish floating batteries. Others are highly picturesque views of the caves in the Rock, which might conjure up the shadowy caverns of John Robert Cozens were it not for the absolute clarity of their every line. Such, if any, was the extent of the "sublime" school's influence on him. He had no wish to sacrifice even one small detail to poetic sentiment or generalization. He left Gibraltar before August 1784, having kept a record of the rainfall for the Royal Society of London, and returned to England with a number of bird specimens.

In the spring of 1786, when he was approaching 50, he began his fourth and last North American tour. The outward journey was broken at Madeira, where he painted a very full water-colour of a "Valley near the Citadel," which is now in a private collection and is perhaps the same picture he exhibited at the Academy in 1793. Then in June and July there followed a period when his ship disembarked artillery companies in the West Indies, while he painted a series of water-colours of Grenada, St. Vincent, Dominica and St. Kitts, all now in the Royal Ontario Museum. In these he reverted to a diagrammatic if very delicate style. The views are often enlivened with charming details from the life of the people: a mother and child walking by a banana plantation or a group of dark-skinned children bathing in the warm sea.

By autumn he was in Quebec, where he began a four-year stint as artillery commander of the garrison. This was a peace-time posting and it evidently afforded him ample time to devote to his art. Here he painted his finest series of water-colours, all but one of which are in the National Gallery of Canada. In them the mature style developed to its point of highest perfection.

It was appropriate that he should begin the series, in 1787, with a *View of Quebec taken near Beauport Ferry* (page 41). This airy panorama sparkling in the sun has in its foreground several

45

continues page 54

47

Château-Richer church, shown at far left, was built about 1680 and rebuilt after its destruction in 1759. The present church has a single belfry dating from 1865. The scene is one of unusual beauty, as Heriot noticed: the "parish church is placed on a bank, immediately behind the chateau [not visible here], and has two spires . . . . Towards the east, a yet happier combination of objects presents itself . . . the church, banks cloathed with foliage, and the lower grounds studded with white cottages." Davies often used Indians as ornamental details in his landscapes, but the view near Pointe-Lévis at left is unusual in that the Indian encampment is made the central subject of the picture. "In the rear of Aubigny," Bouchette writes, "are the heights of Pointe Lévi, where batteries were erected by the Americans. A little below Mr McKenzie's hotel and between it and Pointe aux Peres is a place where the Indians chiefly encamp every summer when they repair to Quebec for the purpose of receiving their annual presents."

This magnificent view of the parade at Quebec
was taken from a point near the gate
of the Château Saint-Louis in 1789.
The artist worked from the site
of the present Dufferin Terrace.
A portion of the Récollet monastery is visible
at left and farther to the right
houses in the Rue Sainte-Anne and the Rue Buade.
Behind them the roof and spires of the cathedral
can be seen. In the left foreground
a dog is pulling a water-cart.
"In many places hereabouts," Kalm notes,
"they use their dogs to fetch water out of the river . . . .
They had neat harness, like horses, and bits
in their mouths. In the cart was a barrel.
The dogs were directed by a boy, who ran behind the cart . . . .
The boys that attend them have great whips."
Davies' boy, true to form, is using a whip,
but he is riding in the cart, not running behind it.

NATIONAL GALLERY OF CANADA

48

*Davies never tired of painting water in movement. This is a view of the Riviere Sault-à-la Puce
near Quebec. Other early travellers admired the scene. Heriot remarks that "the river* la Puce . . .
*by an engaging display of natural attractions, invites the attention of the traveller; it rolls
its current, broken into a refulgent whiteness equalling that of snow, from the summit
of a lofty hill, and afterwards conceals itself midway, behind an intervening eminence
of inferior altitude, cloathed with trees." The scene at right is of a bridge on the same river.
The woods are in autumn colour and in the foreground there are hunters returning from the field,
a man talking to a woman, two men riding a cart and a man hauling a canoe. "The country
is very steep towards the river," as Kalm noticed, "and grows higher as you go farther
from the water . . . . All the country is laid out for corn-fields, meadows, and pastures . . . .
The dwelling-house is commonly built of lime-slates, and generally whitewashed [as here] on
the outside. Many rivulets and brooks roll down the high grounds."*

Above: a view of the Salmon Pool on the Jacques Cartier River. Jacques Cartier wintered at Stadacona in 1535-36 and gave his name to the river and also to a post on the upper road between Montreal and Quebec. The treatment of rock and water are characteristic of the mature Davies style, as are the figures. The couple at right have brought a picnic basket, while others have brought their dogs or just a fishing-rod. The view at right is singularly impressive, with its strong vertical rock-forms, its rich colours and rushing water. The falls are on the Sainte-Anne River above Sainte-Anne-de-Beaupré. The wildness of the scene impressed Bouchette, who described it at length. "A rough path," he says, "conducts the visitor . . . into a most solitary vale of rocks and trees, almost a natural grotto, through the centre of which the stream rushes until it escapes by a narrow channel between the rocks, and continues roaring and tumbling with augmenting velocity. From below there is a striking view of the cataract, which combined with the natural wildness and extraordinary features of the scene defies description; the painter alone could convey to the mind the representation with effect." "Sublimity," Emily Montague writes, "is the characteristic of the western world; the loftiness of the mountains, the grandeur of the lakes and rivers, the majesty of the rocks shaded with a picturesque variety of beautiful trees and shrubs . . . ."

53

Canadiens contentedly walking by the water's edge, and further back the familiar figure of the artist sketching on the bank. Seen across the mouth of the St. Charles River is the distant city with its cathedral and other churches and, at right, a part of the Citadel; all are precisely defined though on a miniature scale. This picture might have inspired Joseph Bouchette's remark that "whoever views the environs of Quebec will acknowledge that as a whole, the prospect is grand, harmonious, and magnificent; and that if taken in detail, every part will please."

Davies set to work to paint the beauty-spots in the neighbourhood of Quebec. *A View of the Falls of Chaudier near Quebec* (page 42), dated 1787, includes another self-portrait (for the first time identified as such) and the picturesque fall on the Chaudière with its jagged rocks, which evoked such rhapsodies as Heriot's "wild diversity . . . brilliance of colours . . . rapidity of motion, the effulgent brightness of the cataracts, and the deep and solemn sound which they emit." To meet the challenge of such scenes as this Davies struck a richer chord of colour, light and shade than ever before.

Maturity is also evident in another water-colour of 1787, *View of Chateau Riche Cape Torment and lower end of the Isle of Orleans* (page 43). But as always he is careful to render most faithfully the many details of the country round the village of Château-Richer and the life of its people: the stone houses with shingled roofs, the timber barns with their thatch-and-board roofs, the little orchards and kitchen-gardens as noted by Kalm in 1749, the big seine-nets in the river and the broad salt marshes that abounded in game birds. Painted the following year, *A View of Chateau Richy Church* (page 46)—Davies' spellings show a characteristic eighteenth-century latitude—shows a church of 1680 with graceful twin spires. In the landscape he bears out Weld's observation that "it was pleasing beyond description to behold one of these villages opening to the view . . . the spires of the churches sparkling through the groves with which they are encircled." The road with its figures is used to create a startling effect of recession into space. It is an effect seen in a number of Paul Sandby's drawings.

Having painted so many Indians as ornaments to his landscapes Davies at last, in 1788, devoted an entire picture to them. *A View near Point Levy Opposite Quebec with an Indian Encampment*

54

(page 47) portrays the place where the bands came to receive their annual bounty.

In 1789 he painted his one and only street scene. The luminous *View of the Parade of Quebec taken near the Chateau Gate* (page 49) shows the Place d'Armes as it appeared 30 years after the bombardment of 1759, all neatly restored. This picture, which is of considerable documentary value, takes in a corner of the old Récollet monastery (the present Anglican cathedral is on the site) with its famous old tree, as well as a water-cart drawn by a dog, the houses in the Rue Sainte-Anne and the Rue Buade and the cathedral about which Bouchette was so condescending: "nothing like taste in design" except for the tower of 1689, which, he said, had an "air of lightness not altogether devoid of beauty."

Then followed a series depicting the natural wonders of the region. The rushing water in *A View on the River La Puce near Quebec* (page 50) seems to epitomize an often-repeated phrase of Heriot, "refulgent whiteness equalling that of snow"; yet this water is somehow solid and immobilized like the glassy paradisal water in C.S. Lewis's *The Great Divorce*. The dense forest, the hunter and his dog, the bear and the deep shadows lend an air of excitement to the scene. This water-colour, and the *View of Bridge on the River La Puce* (page 51) taken "in the fall of the year," surpass eighteenth-century literary descriptions. Kalm on the subject of autumn colours in Canada could rise only to "pale and reddish"; Davies painted them in all their glory. They reappear most beautifully in *A View of the lower part of the falls of St. Anne* (page 53), one of his masterpieces. In the monumental simplicity of its composition and the effective stylization of the rock forms, the fulness of its colour and the delicacy of its line, this picture seems to blend the virtues of European and Chinese painting—though there is no likelihood of any direct oriental influence on Davies' work. Perhaps it was simply that in such a scene as this, as the author of *The History of Emily Montague* declared in 1769, "a landscape-painter might . . . expand his imagination, and find ideas which he will seek in vain in our comparatively little world."

A variation on the theme of waterfalls is provided by a 1790 water-colour of *The Salmon Pool and Subterraneous River at Jacques Cartiere near Quebec* (page 52). The abundance of salmon in the curiously eroded Jacques Cartier River amply justified its popu-

55

continues page 57

This is the same scene on the *La Puce*
as that reproduced on page 50,
but looked at from the opposite direction.
The artist is here looking down the gorge
from farther upstream,
with the St. Lawrence valley
in the background.
Four figures can be seen
in the middle distance
admiring the view.
There are touches of autumn colouring
in the foreground.

56

larity with fishing parties in those days.

A View of the Montmorenci Falls near Quebec (page 59) was "taken in 1790" but is signed and dated 1791. As a composition it is even more boldly conceived than the Sainte-Anne picture. Here for once Davies is outdone by contemporary writers—at least by Emily Montague on the subject of Montmorency: "one of the noblest works of nature: the beauty, the proportion, the solemnity, the wild magnificence of which, surpassing every possible effect of art, impress one strongly with the idea of its Divine Almighty Architect . . . . In short, my dear, I am Montmorenci-mad." Included in this picture is Governor Haldimand's little summer-house, the precarious situation of which, overhanging the falls, held a fatal attraction for the visitor.

An undated *View of the Great Falls on the Outavauis River Lower Canada* (page 58) bears an inscription mentioning Lower Canada, which places it after the passage of the Constitutional Act of 1791 dividing the province into Upper and Lower Canada. It shows the old portage at the Chaudière Falls on the Ottawa River (now in Hull opposite the modern city of Ottawa) which has only recently been rediscovered. *A View on the River La Puce near Quebeck* (page 56), dated 1792, is rich and solid in technique and dark and mysterious in effect. Also from 1792, *The Falls on the Chaudière near Quebec* (page 42) is a view of the scene in the water-colour of 1787 taken from a different angle.

These last four drawings were done after Davies left Quebec in November 1790 and so were completed in England from earlier sketches. After his return he was promoted colonel in 1794 and major-general in 1796. War had broken out again with France, and from 1793 to 1796 he was in command of coastal artillery at Plymouth. Several views of that city and the surrounding country date from the period and are now in private collections.

In 1794 Davies exhibited at the Royal Academy a lost view of the Straits of Malacca, and in 1797 he painted an existing view of Lake Hsi Hu near Hangchow. There is also a drawing of the Whampoa River. These would lead to the conclusion that he accompanied the celebrated Macartney Embassy to China in 1793–94, but for the fact that his name does not appear in the records nor does he mention any such journey in his "Statement of Services." It appears, to judge from one identical title, that he copied engravings   57

continues page 62

Left: the Chaudière Falls on the Ottawa River, taken from one of the small islands in midstream between the modern cities of Ottawa and Hull. This was one of the major portages on the trade route to the interior. "At the portages," Heriot says, "where waterfalls and cataracts oblige them to unload, the men unite in aiding each other to convey the canoes and goods across the land, by carrying the former on the shoulders of six or eight men, and the latter upon the back." Just such a scene can be observed here. Fourteen men are traversing the falls by land, some with packs on their backs, others (two at a time) carrying canoes. The view at right is of the Montmorency Falls near Quebec. General Haldimand, Weld tells us, "was so much delighted with this cataract, that he built a dwelling house close to it . . . . There is also a summer house, situated nearly at the top of the fall, hanging directly over the precipice"—it is just visible here above the crest —"supported by large beams of timber, fixed into the sides of the chasm . . . . The view from hence is tremendously grand. It is said, that the beams whereon this little edifice is erected are in a state of decay, and many persons are fearful of entering into it."

This view of the Chaudière Falls near Quebec was completed in England
from sketches made earlier on the site.
The sketches appear to have been made from a point
farther upstream than the view on page 42.
Note the fisherman at the foot of the falls
and the tiny figures of sightseers at the top of the cliff on the other side.
The luminous view of Montreal at right was painted in 1812,
the year of Davies' death. It is his last water-colour
and was evidently based on studies made much earlier in his career.
Davies had painted Montreal from the south in 1762;
in this view the same buildings can be seen from the north.
In the later work the treatment is more austere
but the eye is as clear, the hand as steady as ever.
Note the Union Jack, the only spot of bright colour, flying over the fort.

made from the drawings of one of Macartney's draughtsmen, William Alexander. Even at this stage of his career he did not feel himself above using the work of others for his own ends.

In 1799 he was appointed colonel-commandant of the Royal Artillery. Two lost views of Newcastle-upon-Tyne, which he exhibited at this time, may indicate that he held a command in the north of England. Two very full water-colours in private hands, the one of Funchal in Madeira (1801) and the other of the River Cobre in Jamaica (1803), may be the products of tours of inspection made in those parts.

By now—Davies was about 60 in 1797—he was an ornithologist of note. Long a student of natural history, he had exhibited plant and animal studies at the Royal Academy and had brought back bird specimens from North America and Gibraltar. In 1770 he had contributed a short paper on the preservation of birds to the Royal Society of London, and in 1781 he had been elected a Fellow, with some of the leading scientists of the day as his sponsors. In 1798 and 1800, at the Linnean Society of London, of which he was also a Fellow, he read papers on birds that had been sent to him from New South Wales.

By this time too he had his own private "museum." In 1781 Dr. John Latham, in the first volume of his monumental work, *General Synopsis of Birds*, warmly acknowledges his "free communication of every knowledge or observation in Natural History in his power."[13] In his *General History of Birds* (1821) Latham pays posthumous tribute to Davies, "from whose faithful pencil I have been furnished with many exact representations of new subjects, taken from the different Ornithological collections of his friends, independent of those in his own well-chosen cabinet of subjects in Natural History."[14] Five signed drawings are to be found in the Latham Collection at the Natural History Museum, London.

By 1803 Davies seems to have been virtually retired. He drops out of sight except for a bird drawing dated 1805 and a farewell appearance at the Royal Academy in 1806. At his death at Blackheath near Woolwich, on the 16th of March, 1812, he left his wife Mary, a son George and a daughter Maria, who married into one of the other military families of the place.

Earlier that year he had painted his last picture of Canada. Based on earlier sketches, the view of *Montreal* (page 61) from the mountain is a masterpiece of composition and execution. Each successive plane is linked to the next by lines that penetrate space in a most accomplished and convincing way. The foreground is powerfully defined by great weathered boulders on the mountainside. The middle distance, framed by trees, is dotted with peaceful farms that offer a contrast to the rocky foreground. Beyond lies the city, compact within its walls, its every building precisely drawn and evenly lighted. The background is closed by St. Helen's Island and the conical hills of the south shore. Davies' vision of Canada remained strong and fresh to the end.

[1]Ellis Waterhouse, *Painting in Britain 1530–1790* (London, 1953), p. 238. In this introduction I have incorporated, with permission, much of the substance of a paper read at the Royal Society of Canada in June 1971 and published in the *Transactions* for that year.

[2]Kathleen M. Fenwick, "Thomas Davies—Soldier and Painter of Eighteenth-Century Canada," *Canadian Art*, XIII (1956), 274.

[3]*Ibid.*, p. 274.

[4]There is at present no trace of the 126 bird drawings at Knowsley, mentioned in F.C. Sawyer, "Notes on Some Original Drawings of Birds Used by Dr. John Latham," *Journal of the Society for the Bibliography of Natural History*, II (1943–52), 175.

[5]"Christie's Back to King Street," *Financial Times*, 21 October, 1953.

[6]F. St. George Spendlove, *The Face of Early Canada* (Toronto, 1958), p. 15.

[7]Fenwick, *loc. cit.* and C.P. Stacey, "Officer of Rank and Talent," *Canadian Art,* XIII (1956), 274–76, 300.

[8]See his "Lieutenant General Thomas Davies, Soldier, Painter and Naturalist," in the catalogue of the Davies exhibition, National Gallery of Canada, 1972. Among the others who helped in this undertaking Major R.G. Bartelot of the Royal Artillery Institution, Woolwich, is most to be thanked. Mr. Paul R. Huey, Senior Historical Archeologist, State of New York, gave helpful information on Davies' view of Greenbush, and Mr. D.L. Serventy of Nedlands, Western Australia, first drew my attention to Davies as a bird illustrator.

[9]This drawing is said to be a replica by Davies of a lost original (R.H. Murdock, *The Brome-Walton Family* [Woolwich, 1895], p. 53).

[10]Quoted in Murdock, pp. 53–57.

[11]Not reproduced in this portfolio.

[12]Not reproduced in this portfolio.

[13]John Latham, *General Synopsis of Birds* (2 vols., London, 1781), I. 100.

[14]John Latham, *A General History of Birds* (2 vols., London, 1821), I. x–xi.

PRIMARY SOURCES

Davies, Thomas. Letter to John Ellis, 12 March, 1770, on a method of preserving birds; read (with changes) at the Royal Society of London and published in *Philosophical Transactions* (1770), pp. 184–87; original in the library of the Royal Society, London. Two letters to Lord Amherst, Fort Knyphausen, 5, 17 July, 1778; originals in the Public Record Office (Amherst Papers), microfilms in the Public Archives of Canada. Letter to Sir Joseph Banks, August 1784, about rainfall at Gibraltar; library of the Royal Society, London. Letter to Samuel More, 6 February, 1792, mentioning settlements on the west coast of North America; Royal Society of Arts, London. "An Account of the Jumping Mouse of Canada. Dipus Canadensis," *Transactions of the Linnean Society*, V (1798), 155–57, with a colour engraving. "Account of a New Species of Muscicapa, from New South Wales," *Transactions of the Linnean Society*, IV (1798), 240–42, with a colour engraving. Unsigned letter, ca. 1799–1812, to Dr. John Latham, postmarked Blackheath, about two birds with similar heads, illustrated with two drawings; attached to verso of drawing No. 203, Latham Collection, Zoological Library, Museum of Natural History, London. "Description of Menura superba, a Bird of New South Wales," *Transactions of the Linnean Society*, VI (1802), 207–10, with a colour engraving. Unsigned letter to Dr. John Latham, Blackheath, 7 March, 1803, about an Indian bird; attached to verso of drawing No. 108, Latham Collection. "Statement of Services," quoted in R.H. Murdock, *The Brome-Walton Family* (Woolwich, 1895), pp. 53–57 as being "from an original manuscript."

Duncan, Francis. *History of the Royal Regiment of Artillery*. London, 1879.

Ford, Worthington C. *British Officers Serving in the American Revolution*. Brooklyn, 1897.

Gentleman's Magazine, April 1812. Obituary notice.

Kane, John. *List of Officers of the Royal Regiment of Artillery*. Woolwich, 1900.

Laws, M.E.S. *Battery Records of the Royal Artillery*. Woolwich, 1952.

Mathews, G.M. and Iredale, T. "Forgotten Bird-Artists and an Old-Time Ornithologist," *Austral Avian Record*, IV (1920), 114–21.

Quebec Gazette, 1787–90. References to Davies *passim*.

SECONDARY SOURCES: THOMAS DAVIES

Fenwick, Kathleen M. "Thomas Davies—Soldier and Painter of Eighteenth-Century Canada," *Canadian Art,* XIII (1956), 271–74 .

Hubbard, R.H., editor. *Thomas Davies.* An exhibition prepared by the National Gallery of Canada with a forward by Jean Sutherland Boggs and a biographical essay by C.P. Stacey. Ottawa, 1972.

—— "Thomas Davies, Gunner and Artist," *Transactions of the Royal Society of Canada,* 4:IX (1971), 342–49.

National Gallery of Canada. *Engagement Calendar: Water-Colours by Thomas Davies,* with notes by W.S.A. Dale. Ottawa, 1967.

Stacey, C.P. "Officer of Rank and Talent," *Canadian Art,* XIII (1956), 274–75, 300.

SECONDARY SOURCES: DESCRIPTIONS OF NORTH AMERICA

Amherst, Jeffery. *The Journal of Jeffery Amherst,* edited by J. Clarence Webster. Toronto, 1931.

Bouchette, Joseph. *A Topographical Description of the Province of Lower Canada.* London, 1815.

—— *The British Dominions in North America.* London, 1832.

—— *A Topographical Dictionary of the Province of Lower Canada.* London, 1832.

[Brooke, Frances]. *The History of Emily Montague.* London, 1769.

Heriot, George. *Travels through the Canadas.* London, 1807.

Kalm, Peter. *Travels into North America,* translated by John Reinhold Forster. 3 vols., London, 1770–71.

—— *The America of 1750: Peter Kalm's Travels in North America,* revised and edited by Adolph B. Benson with a translation of new material from Kalm's diary notes. New York, 1937.

Knox, John. *An Historical Journal of the Campaign in North America,* edited by Arthur G. Doughty. 3 vols., Toronto, 1914–16.

Monckton, Robert. *The Northcliffe Collection:* Monckton papers. Ottawa, 1926.

Rochefoucault, Francois duc de la. *Travels through the United States of North America.* London, 1799.

Weld, Isaac. *Travels through the States of North America and the Provinces of Upper and Lower Canada.* 3 vols., London, 1799.

Williamson, George. Papers: microfilm in the Public Archives of Canada.

Library of Congress Catalogue Card No. 72–77036

ISBN 0 88750 068 4

Book design by Michael Macklem

Printed in Hong Kong by Serasia Limited

PUBLISHED IN CANADA BY OBERON PRESS